YOU CHO

FOUNDING
UNITED STATES

RESISTING
BRITISH RULE
An Interactive American Revolution Adventure

by Elizabeth Raum

Consultant:
Richard Bell, PhD
Associate Professor of History
University of Maryland, College Park

CAPSTONE PRESS
a capstone imprint

SOMERSET CO. LIBRARY
BRIDGEWATER, N.J. 08807

You Choose Books are published by Capstone Press,
1710 Roe Crest Drive, North Mankato, Minnesota 56003
www.mycapstone.com

Copyright © 2019 by Capstone Press, a Capstone imprint. All rights reserved.
No part of this publication may be reproduced in whole or in part, or stored in a
retrieval system, or transmitted in any form or by any means, electronic, mechanical,
photocopying, recording, or otherwise, without written permission of the publisher.

Library of Congress Cataloging-in-Publication Data
Library of Congress Cataloging-in-Publication data is available on the Library of
Congress website.

978-1-5435-1541-1 (library binding)
978-1-5435-1548-0 (paperback)

Editorial Credits
Adrian Vigliano, editor; Bobbie Nuytten, designer;
Kelly Garvin, media researcher; Kathy McColley, production specialist

Photo Credits
Bridgeman Images/Troiani, Don (b.1949) / Private Collection, cover; Getty
Images: Encyclopaedia Britannica/Contributor, 68, Hulton Archive/Stringer, 24;
North Wind Picture Archive, 7, 10, 16, 37, 40, 47, 59, 72, 78, 82, 89, 94, 100, 104;
Science Source/Library of Congress, 61; Shutterstock: A-R-T, 53, 71, Everett-Art,
52, Everett Historical, 65

Artistic elements: Shutterstock: Abstractor, photka

Printed and bound in Canada.
PA020

Table of Contents

ABOUT YOUR ADVENTURE

YOU are living during a time of change. The American colonies are still ruled by the British. But conflicts are increasing, and colonial leaders are ready to challenge King George III and the British Parliament. Is there any chance of avoiding war? Will you be caught in the middle of the conflict?

In this book you'll explore how the choices people made meant the difference between life and death. The events you'll experience happened to real people.

Chapter One sets the scene. Then you choose which path to read. Follow the directions at the bottom of each page. The choices you make will change your outcome. After you finish your path, go back and read the others for new perspectives and more adventures.

YOU CHOOSE the path
you take through history.

American colonists protested unpopular acts passed by the British Parliament, such as the Stamp Act.

CHAPTER 1

COLONY IN REVOLT

The year is 1773, a time of increasing uncertainty in the American colonies. Some towns and cities have formed rebel groups called the Sons of Liberty. In Philadelphia the local Sons of Liberty hold a mass meeting.

Like many other American colonists, Philadelphians are sick of taxes. The British Parliament has just enacted the Tea Act, the latest in a series of harsh taxes. The Tea Act allows the colonies to buy tea from one British company alone, the East India Company. On top of that, the tea will be taxed heavily. Many colonists believe it's an instance of unfair taxes. They believe the British take what they want in taxes but give little back.

Turn the page.

Those attending the Sons of Liberty meeting in Philadelphia declare that anyone who imports tea is "an enemy to his country." Many colonists plan to make do with homemade "Liberty Tea." It's made from red root bush, red sumac berries, raspberries, and various herbs. It's not as tasty as imported tea, but it's a small price to pay to defy the British.

In New York City, the Sons of Liberty make plans to turn away any tea ships that attempt to dock. Thanks to a storm that sends the tea ships off course, they don't have to do anything.

Things are different in Boston. In December three tea ships sail into Boston Harbor. On December 6, 1773, Boston's patriot leaders hold a rally. About 8,000 people attend. Later that night 50 men board one of the tea ships and dump 90,000 pounds of tea into the water. Boston's rebels pretend to be Mohawk Indians. They dress in black and paint their faces red. But no one is fooled.

Samuel Adams, one of the patriot leaders, writes an article for the *Boston Gazette*. In it he claims that the tea dumping is just the beginning of a war against Great Britain. The next day the Sons of Liberty hold rallies in New York and Philadelphia.

Many colonists cheer on the tea protest. Others, who remain loyal to Great Britain, are disgusted. Parliament is outraged. Its members pass a series of rulings called the Coercive Acts. The news of the Coercive Acts reaches Boston in the spring of 1774. Colonists call them the Intolerable Acts. Colonial leaders begin planning the First Continental Congress.

Everyone is choosing sides. It's time for you to make some decisions too.

To go to Boston as resistance to the British continues to grow, turn to page 11.

To go to Philadelphia as the First Continental Congress forms, turn to page 41.

To serve as an express rider, turn to page 73.

Printed posters called handbills were an important form of communication among colonists. Before the Revolutionary War some posted handbills warned colonists against buying British goods.

The true Sons of Liberty

And Supporters of the Non-Importation Agreement,

ARE determined to rēſent any the leaſt Inſult or Menace offer'd to any one or more of the ſeveral Committees appointed by the Body at Faneuil-Hall, and chaſtiſe any one or more of them as they deſerve ; and will alſo ſupport the Printers in any Thing the Committees ſhall deſire them to print.

☞AS a Warning to any one that ſhall affront as aforeſaid, upon ſure Information given, one of theſe Advertiſements will be poſted up at the Door or Dwelling-Houſe of the Offender.

CHAPTER 2

CHOOSING SIDES

Your father storms inside, holding the latest edition of the *Boston Gazette*. "King George has ordered the Port of Boston closed until we pay for the tea that was dumped into the harbor. That's not going to happen. Not now. Not ever!"

Father is a member of the Sons of Liberty. Patriot leaders Samuel Adams, John Hancock, and Dr. Joseph Warren are among his friends. They've agreed not to follow British orders.

"What will we do?" your mother asks. Father builds and repairs ships. If the harbor closes, he'll have no work.

"We'll go to Lexington. My brother Harvey has room, and he's always saying he needs help with the farm. The children will be safe there.

Turn the page.

Soon we'll have so many British soldiers in Boston that the streets will glow with their red uniforms."

"Lexington?" You're stunned. "But Grandfather has asked me to help in his store."

"Grandfather is growing old and careless," Mother says. "You could look after him. The extra money will come in handy."

Father rubs his chin. "I'd prefer you to come with us, but you're nearly grown. You decide."

To go to Lexington, go to page 13.

To stay in Boston, turn to page 15.

It's hard to give up the offer of a paying job, but you decide to stay with the family. Luckily, you enjoy farm work. You plant crops, milk cows, and help your cousin Richard build a new hog shelter.

News from Boston is discouraging. King George has appointed General Thomas Gage, a British army officer, as the governor of Massachusetts.

You and your father join the local militia. You go target shooting with cousin Richard. He can get off three shots a minute. Soon you're matching his time.

"We're lucky to have hunting rifles," Richard says. "There's a shortage of weapons. We used to get guns from Great Britain, but we can't do that now."

Some men bring pitchforks to militia drills. The pitchforks won't do much good against British rifles, but in close combat, they'll slow the enemy.

Turn the page.

You drill twice a week. Captain Parker says every town is gathering whatever powder, cannons, and ammunition it can. Townspeople are hiding these supplies from British troops.

On September 1, 1774, a horse gallops into the yard. Father and Uncle Harvey rush outside.

"The British robbed our ammunition!" the rider says. "In Somerville the British broke into the powder house. When the townspeople resisted, British soldiers fired into the crowd. Six dead. Meet at the town square to march to Cambridge. Captain Parker's orders."

Father, Uncle Harvey, and Richard run for their guns. You jump up too, but Mother holds you back. "No," she says. "Someone has to stay to protect us."

You look to your father for guidance. He shakes his head. The decision is yours.

To go to Cambridge, turn to page 18.

To stay at the farm, turn to page 20.

It's not just the money that keeps you in Boston. Grandfather needs you. His shop sells British goods such as fabrics, buttons, and London fashions to the wealthy ladies of Boston. Grandfather is a loyalist. He wants America to keep close ties to England. "We trade with Great Britain," he says. "America needs England's business."

Father disagrees. "We'd be better off on our own, without taxes and unfair laws."

Mother says little. She wants to keep the family safe. "War is not good for families," she says.

As far as you can tell, Grandfather and his loyalist friends love America just as much as Father does. They simply favor working with King George rather than against him.

You pack a small bag and go to Grandfather's. A maid shows you to a third-floor room. From there you can see much of Boston.

Turn the page.

Thomas Gage became an unpopular governor with many colonists as he enforced the Intolerable Acts and the closure of the Port of Boston.

On May 13, 1774, British General Thomas Gage arrives in Boston with orders to close the city's port. Gage is both governor and military commander. Many people leave Boston. By mid-July only a third of the city's population remains. Luckily, loyalist shoppers still come to Grandfather's shop.

By the spring of 1775, you know the business almost as well as Grandfather does. You stock the shelves and help customers. Grandfather often sends you on errands.

To go to General Gage's house, go to page 17.

To go to Henry Knox's bookstore, turn to page 19.

General Gage lives at Province House. A maid answers the door.

"Who is it?" a woman calls from a back room.

"A delivery boy," says the maid.

Mrs. Gage comes to the door. Several children follow her. Before you can hand over the package, General Gage comes home.

"Papa!" the children shout. Gage and another British officer brush past and slip into a side room.

"Wait here while I get your payment," Mrs. Gage says.

Suddenly you hear a loud commotion and a scream from a nearby room.

To go see what happened, turn to page 25.

To wait as instructed, turn to page 30.

Uncle Harvey stays at the farm. You march to Cambridge with the militia. It turns out that the attack on the powder house is a false alarm.

"There were thousands of us from all over New England," Richard tells Uncle Harvey when you return. "We showed General Gage that if he attacks, we'll fight back."

Soon people call what happened in Cambridge the Powder Alarm. Fall and winter pass quickly. Soon it's spring, time to prepare for planting.

Early on April 19, an alarm rider gallops into the yard. "The British are coming!" he says. Father takes you aside and tells you that if fighting occurs, a man's first duty is to protect the women and children. One of you must stand guard at home. But someone must ride on to Woburn to alert the militia there.

To stand guard, turn to page 22.

To ride to Woburn, turn to page 36.

18

Knox's store, the London Book Shop, is just down the street from General Gage's headquarters at Province House. Grandfather buys all his books from Knox's store. He prefers to trade with other loyalists, such as the Knox family.

It only takes a minute to fetch the book Grandfather ordered. As you leave you meet your friend Jacob Jones, an apprentice shoemaker.

Jacob is troubled. "I overheard British officers talking about a raid on Concord," he says.

"Concord?" you ask. That's not far from Lexington, where your family has gone. Father and Uncle Harvey are active in the Lexington militia.

You talk for a while longer. Jacob is a patriot. You've heard it all before from your father. But the more Jacob talks, the more you agree with him that the British are taking advantage of the colonists.

To side with the loyalists, turn to page 26.

To side with the patriots, turn to page 33.

"I'll stay," you say. Your mother bows her head in relief. Your father nods. He approves. It's hard to see the others march off, but they are back before nightfall.

"False alarm," Father says. "No one was killed. The only powder left in the powder house belonged to the British."

Father gets reports from the First Continental Congress, which is meeting in Philadelphia. "The Congress supports a boycott of British goods," he says. "We can't import them or use them. We can't send goods to Great Britain, either. And they are trying to convince King George to change his policies."

Uncle Harvey shakes his head. "He's not likely to do so."

Father agrees. "So we prepare for war. Congress also says local militia companies should meet, arm themselves, and drill."

One day Captain Parker, head of the Lexington militia, says that John Hancock and Samuel Adams are in Lexington staying with Reverend Jonas Clark. "We must keep them safe. General Gage wants to arrest them. He'd love to imprison our leaders. If you hear the church bells ring, meet at Lexington Green."

At 2:00 a.m. on April 19 an alarm rider shouts, "The British are coming!" You leap out of bed, dress, and rush downstairs.

"Not so fast," Father says. "This may be another false alarm. I plan to wait until I hear the church bells."

Richard is on his way out the door.

To go with Richard, turn to page 23.

To wait, turn to page 32.

You agree to guard the women and children. You watch as the others rush to Lexington Green. Mother is nervous. "We can't stay here. The British will search the houses," she says.

"The woods?" Aunt Emma suggests.

The women agree. "We'll leave at sunrise." They load a basket with bread and cheese, and hand you a jug of milk. At dawn, they follow you into the woods. You find a mossy patch of meadow surrounded by trees. The women spread blankets down.

Shots ring out in the distance.

"I have to go!" The woods swallow your words as you run toward town.

Turn to page 28.

It only takes a minute to grab your rifle and head to town. The town looks deserted.

"Where is everyone?" you ask Captain Parker.

"They're gathering at Buckman's Tavern," the captain says.

You follow him there. The tavern has a direct view of the green. Around 5 a.m. the sun rises. Parker sends Thaddeus Bowman on horseback to look for the British. He returns minutes later.

"They're coming!" shouts Bowman.

You swarm out of the tavern and form one long line of 80 men across the green.

The British march straight for you. "Huzza! Huzza! Huzza!" they yell.

"Let the troops pass," Parker orders.

The British pound forward, moving closer and closer.

Turn the page.

At the Battle of Lexington, a small number of militiamen faced off against about 700 British troops.

24

"Disperse!" Parker shouts. "Do not fire!"

The British officers are yelling too. Some of the militiamen run. You stand your ground.

A shot rings out. Who shot? You don't know, but more shots follow.

"Cease fire!"

"Run!"

Turn to page 28.

You follow the noise and see two children playing with a puppy. When you return to the hallway, the maid hands you an envelope for Grandfather.

At home you find Dr. Benjamin Church visiting. "I was telling your grandfather that he should consider leaving Boston. Several of the soldiers are suffering from smallpox, diphtheria, or various other contagious diseases. It's not wise to stay."

Turn to page 37.

After thinking for a few minutes, you say, "I know that much of what you say is right. But if the colonies present their concerns to King George, he's bound to listen," you say. "How can the colonies protect themselves without help from the British? We have neither army nor navy. If the Spanish or French were to attack, we'd be at their mercy."

Jacob shakes his head. "Be careful," he warns. "It's dangerous to be on the wrong side."

Later you talk to Grandfather. "The Continental Congress has sent a letter of grievances to the king," he says. "The king will stop this nonsense."

Trade begins to fall off. Ships bring British soldiers, not goods. They camp on Boston Common and spend days drilling and training. It looks as if they're preparing for war.

On April 19 several regiments march out of Boston before dawn. That night after dark you look out your window and see dozens of lanterns bobbing near the docks. You open the window. In the chilly night air you hear screams of men in pain.

The news is terrible. "Our troops were ambushed by militia on the way home from Lexington and Concord," Grandfather says.

His accountant rushes through the door. "Have you heard the news?" he asks. Before anyone can answer, he adds, "Thousands of country people are marching to Boston. They are camping across from Charlestown Neck and in Roxbury and Cambridge. They may storm the city. It's not safe here."

Turn to page 37.

White smoke from the gunfire is blinding. It's difficult to know where to go.

You look toward Buckman's Tavern. Militiamen often gather there. It is next to Lexington Green, where they trained. Now the green is a battlefield.

Someone fires from a first-floor window of Buckman's Tavern. You see another flash of gunfire from a second-floor window.

A British commander yells, "Cease fire!" but the shooting continues.

To enter Buckman's, go to page 29.

To join the fighting, turn to page 38.

You run toward the tavern. Two men approach from the other direction. They're not in British uniforms. "Give us a hand," one of them says.

The face is familiar. It's Paul Revere.

"We've come for John Hancock's trunk," Revere says. "He left it here, and it's full of valuable papers."

"Upstairs!" the innkeeper shouts. "First room on the right."

You follow Revere and his companion, John Lowell, to the room. You help them carry the heavy trunk downstairs, across the far side of the green, and into a waiting cart.

Then you rush back to the green.

Turn to page 38.

29

A nanny rushes by to help. You wait by the door. You overhear what the British officer is saying to General Gage.

"A sudden blow struck now or within a fortnight would upset all their plans."

You can't hear Gage's response, but the officer adds something about "the cannon at Concord."

The maid gives you an envelope for your grandfather. You take it and leave, but you can't stop thinking about the conversation. "Concord?" you think. "That's near Lexington." You must warn Father, but first you must tell Grandfather that you're going to join the family.

Grandfather begs you to wait a week or two. "I'm going to visit my brother on the northern island of Nova Scotia. Wait until I leave?"

You agree. Grandfather books passage on a British ship. You pack your bags, but it's too late.

You learn that British soldiers have marched on Lexington and Concord. The soldiers return to Boston, battered and bloody. You wonder if the colonists are in even worse condition.

You hurry to Lexington and learn that Uncle Harvey died of a British bullet. Father is wounded. He'll recover, but he won't be able to work for many months.

"They fired the first shot," Father says. "Attacked us for no reason."

"I'll fight in your place," you promise. You join the militia, and when George Washington arrives to command the Continental Army, you sign up. You won't give up until the British do.

THE END
To follow another path, turn to page 9.
To read the conclusion, turn to page 101.

Shortly after midnight the bells ring.

"It's time!" Father shouts.

By the time you reach the green, the battle is nearly over. Before you fire, you look around and see Uncle Harvey lying on a patch of bloody grass. You run to him. As you lift him in your arms he says, "Tell your Aunt Emma . . ."

You're carrying him toward the tavern when something stings your leg. You collapse at the tavern door and realize you've been shot. The wound is serious. You recover, but you'll never fight again. Many years later you tell your grandchildren that you were there when the first shots of the Revolutionary War were fired.

32

THE END

To follow another path, turn to page 9.
To read the conclusion, turn to page 101.

You attended some of the Sons of Liberty meetings with Father. You listened but you didn't really understand. Jacob explains the problem in his own words. Suddenly everything Father has been saying makes sense. "I'm with you," you tell Jacob.

"Meet tonight at the Green Dragon," Jacob says. It's a well-known Boston tavern.

After dinner you say goodnight to Grandfather and go to the Green Dragon. Jacob introduces you to a group of about 30 workers. They are carpenters, brick makers, candle makers, boat builders, gunsmiths, and shopkeepers. "We are all patriots. You'll have to swear on the Bible never to reveal what we say," Jacob tells you.

"To anyone?" you ask.

Turn the page.

Jacob smiles. "Oh, you can tell John Hancock, Samuel Adams, Dr. Joseph Warren, and Dr. Benjamin Church. We trust them. Will you swear to keep our secrets?"

You put your hand on the Bible. "I swear."

They've been spying on the British for months now. "Every bit of information helps," Jacob says. Paul Revere, who is head of the group, nods agreement. You think of Grandfather's store. The soldiers who enter there talk freely. Maybe you'll hear something worth reporting.

More troops arrive in Boston in March 1775. In early April you hear rumors of raids on the towns outside Boston.

"They're trying to steal our cannons and musket powder," Jacob says.

One April night the steady beat of soldiers marching through the streets wakes you. You fall back to sleep. It's the next day before you hear that the British marched on Lexington and Concord. Patriots such as Paul Revere and Billy Dawes warned the towns. Militia units were waiting when the British arrived. The first shots were fired at Lexington. The British pushed on toward Concord—more shots, more deaths, and finally the British retreated. By day's end 19 British officers and 250 British soldiers were dead or wounded. American losses totaled 90.

"We've won the first battle," Jacob says. It's an encouraging victory.

It's bad news for Grandfather. He leaves Boston. You move to Lexington, join the militia, and fight for independence.

THE END

To follow another path, turn to page 9.
To read the conclusion, turn to page 101.

You saddle a fresh horse and ride to Woburn to alert the militia.

"John Hancock and Samuel Adams arrived last night," Sergeant Munroe of the militia tells you. "Paul Revere and John Lowell brought them from Lexington. Hancock wanted to stay and fight, but Adams convinced him not to. It's a good thing too," Munroe adds. "Hancock is far more useful to us as a leader than as a foot soldier."

You go with the militia and march toward Concord. By the time you arrive, the battle is over. But there's still time to strike against the British. You follow them on the road back to Boston.

36

THE END

To follow another path, turn to page 9.
To read the conclusion, turn to page 101.

"I agree," Grandfather says. "I'll stay with my brother. There's a ship leaving tonight for the northern island of Nova Scotia. We'll be safe there." Grandfather staggers as he stands up. "Come with me," he pleads. "I fear I cannot go alone."

You go to Nova Scotia. It is months before you are able to contact your family. War is raging. There is no way to return. It will be years before you see them again.

Hundreds of militiamen parted with their families to fight back against British troops at the Battle of Concord.

THE END

To follow another path, turn to page 9.
To read the conclusion, turn to page 101.

You fire your rifle, reload, and fire again.

A nearby militiaman grabs your sleeve. "Run!" he says. "It's what Captain Parker ordered."

You follow him. He dives over a stone wall and hides behind it. You do too.

When you peer over the wall, you see that shots are coming from the tavern.

British drums beat. The ranks form again and the British march on.

As the smoke clears, you see militiamen lying on the green. Some are dead and others are wounded.

"We've lost eight men," Captain Parker says. "We must avenge them." He gathers the militia's remaining force, about 140 men, and says, "Let's go!"

He takes the militia to the hill that looms above the road back to Boston. "Hide yourselves," he says. "When the British pass below, attack!"

You aren't the only militia company firing on the retreating British. At day's end you return to the farm.

"We gave them a good fight," Richard says. "At least the British know we don't give up. We'll fight until America is ours."

THE END

To follow another path, turn to page 9.
To read the conclusion, turn to page 101.

Patriotic colonists did whatever they could to avoid buying British goods. Some families spun their own yarn so they would not need to buy British cloth.

CHAPTER 3

OVERHEARD IN PHILADELPHIA

On June 1, 1774, your family goes to church even though it's Wednesday. Many churches are holding special meetings in response to the closing of the Port of Boston. "It's a terrible ruling that the British Parliament made," Father says. "With the port closed, the people of Boston will be cut off from supplies." He is a patriot. He says that British laws and taxes are unfair.

Father is the proprietor of the City Tavern. He says it's the newest and most elegant tavern in all of America. You're proud of him. Father knows many important people. They drink coffee, eat dinner, and hold important meetings at the City Tavern.

Turn the page.

Father tells you about another protest. Local clubs for mechanics, merchants, and others will not celebrate King George's birthday this year. "They're angry at the king for his treatment of Boston," he says. Last year Philadelphia celebrated the king's June 4 birthday by ringing church bells throughout the city. Ships flew colorful flags, and huge bonfires lit the night sky. This year not a single bell will ring.

Not everyone in Philadelphia agrees with Father. Your friend Rebecca and her parents are loyal to Britain. Some of your neighbors haven't chosen sides yet.

Father goes to meetings at the Philosophical Hall, Carpenters' Hall, and the State House yard to discuss how to help Boston. "We voted to collect donations to help people there," he reports.

"I will ask the neighbors," Mother says. "We must all do our part. This family will not buy British goods."

Your older sisters, Sara and Molly, groan. "What about clothing? We can still buy British fashions, can't we?"

Mother is firm. "No, we will card wool and spin our own fabric. Then we'll make our garments of wool. Wool is practical."

"It's itchy!" Sara says. She likes wearing silk gowns.

You offer to help.

To collect money for Boston, turn to page 44.

To card and spin wool, turn to page 45.

You go with Mother when she collects donations for Boston. Many want to help.

"Let's not ask here," you say, when you reach Rebecca's house. "Rebecca told me that Boston deserves to be punished."

"Her parents may be more fair minded," Mother says hopefully.

Rebecca and her mother answer the door, but they refuse to give. "The king will reopen the port as soon as the people of Boston pay for the ruined tea," says Rebecca's mother.

Mother bids them farewell, and you both leave. Rebecca stares at you through her window. Then she sticks out her tongue!

Oh, it's tempting to make a face at Rebecca. But it's not something a good friend should do.

To make a face at Rebecca, turn to page 48.

To ignore her, turn to page 54.

Mother gives you a bag of sheep's wool. It's dusty and dirty. Some of it is matted.

"We have to clean it," Mother says.

You scrub the wool in a big bucket and let it dry.

"Next, we'll use hand carders to separate the wool," Mother explains.

You place some wool on the carder and then pull a second carder through the wool to separate the strands. When you are done, the wool is ready to be made into fabric.

"It takes practice," Mother says. Over time you become good at it. Mother is proud. "Now we won't depend on the British for cloth. We'll make our own."

By late August the delegates to the Continental Congress arrive in Philadelphia.

Turn the page.

On September 5 Father reports that they met at the City Tavern. "They voted to hold Congress in Carpenters' Hall," he says. "The Congress will keep us busy. They'll come to the tavern for coffee, dinners, and discussions. Just today I overheard Richard Henry Lee of Virginia talking with several others about the huge number of people the Congress represents. That's quite a responsibility."

"Where will the delegates stay?" Mother asks.

"Several are boarding in private homes. The Massachusetts delegates are at Mrs. Yard's Stone House opposite the tavern. They've become friendly with the Virginia delegates," Father says. "It's odd, I suppose. The Virginia delegates are wealthy men who own large plantations. The Massachusetts men are middle class. But they get along well. Perhaps it's because they share a common cause."

Carpenters' Hall was a brand new building in Philadelphia when the Continental Congress met there in 1774.

"Anger at the king?" you ask.

"Yes," he says. "I heard Patrick Henry say that he is 'not a Virginian, but an American.'"

The next few weeks are busy. You card wool, spend time on your lessons, and do errands for Mother. One day an elderly neighbor, Mrs. Kelly, stops by. "The boy who delivers eggs for me is ill. Will you help?" she asks.

To deliver eggs to Mrs. Chew, turn to page 50.

To deliver them to Mrs. Yard's Stone House, turn to page 67.

You wrinkle your nose and stick out your tongue at Rebecca.

"What are you doing?" Mother asks.

"She did it first," you say.

Mother walks fast when she is angry. You struggle to keep up. When you get home, she tells you to sit at the kitchen table, and then she disappears. A moment later she returns with paper, a pen, and a book. The book is Mother's favorite, *Poor Richard's Almanack*, by Benjamin Franklin. Franklin is in Great Britain now representing the colonies, but he grew up in Boston. He has a home in Philadelphia.

"I'll be knitting," Mother says. "You will find three of Mr. Franklin's sayings that apply to your behavior. Write them down and bring them to me."

You begin reading.

An hour later, you hand Mother the list:

None but the well-bred man knows how to confess a fault, or acknowledge himself in an error.

Wink at small faults—remember thou hast great ones.

Wise Men learn by others' harms; Fools by their own.

"What have you learned?" Mother asks.

"I was wrong to treat Rebecca unkindly, even though she . . ." Mother's stern look causes you to stop speaking. "I will do better next time."

Mother smiles and hugs you. "I fear that difficult times are coming. It is not wise to make enemies of our friends. We must try to get along."

The next day Rebecca passes by carrying a basket.

To ignore her, turn to page 54.

To run outside, turn to page 57.

49

Mrs. Chew lives in a big house on Third Street. You knock on the kitchen door. Mrs. Chew's head cook peeks out the door. "I thought you'd never come," she says. She takes the basket of eggs and sets it on a shelf.

The cooks and kitchen maids are hard at work. One cook is stirring turtle soup. Another is beating the eggs, milk, and sugar for flummery pudding. Another is making whipped syllabubs, a frothy drink made of cream with cider added. You peer over another's shoulder and see that she is making a fruit fool. She's folding stewed gooseberries into sweet custard.

"Off with you," the cook says. "The guests will be here soon. We're having the gentlemen from Virginia and Massachusetts as well as Dr. Shippen from right here in Philadelphia. Since Mr. Chew is the chief justice of the province, it is his duty to entertain these out-of-town guests."

Thinking about the food, you forget to look where you're going. You run smack into a rather short, plump gentleman.

"Oh, my," he says. "I hope you are not injured."

"No, sir," you say. "I was just making a delivery for my mother."

"And who might she be?" he asks.

"Susanna Smith is her name," you say. "My father is Daniel Smith."

"The proprietor of the City Tavern?"

You nod.

"He is a fine gentleman. He has treated us well. I am John Adams, at your service." He removes his hat and bows.

Turn the page.

John Adams served as the first vice president of the United States. He was also the country's second president.

After a pause Adams says, "I am thinking that the young ladies of Pennsylvania and those of Massachusetts have much in common. I have a daughter back in Braintree, Massachusetts, who is about your age. We call her Nabby. Would you do me the honor of writing to her?"

A few days later, Father hands you a slip of paper with Nabby's address. "It's up to you whether to write a letter," he says. "Asa asked if you can help him at the stable."

To write the letter, go to page 53.

To go to the stable, turn to page 63.

It's not easy to write to a complete stranger.
You ask your sisters for help.

"Tell her about me," Sara says.

"Tell her about Philadelphia," Molly suggests.

That's a good idea.

Dear Nabby,

Your father suggested I write to you. He says we can be friends even though we live far apart. I am 11 years old. I live in Philadelphia. It is the biggest city in America. We have about 40,000 people. Your father and the other delegates are meeting at Carpenters' Hall. It's new. Many trade groups meet there when Congress is not in town.

There are many Quakers in Philadelphia. Quakers, or the Society of Friends, want peace, not war. There are loyalists here too. My family and I are patriots. Father says we may have war with Great Britain if King George doesn't listen to Congress. Please tell me about life in Massachusetts.

Your Philadelphia friend.

To try to give the letter to Father, turn to page 59.

To give it to Mr. Adams, turn to page 62.

You recall Father's words: "Many people support the British. I fear that many friends will turn against one another. Let us not do so."

You want to keep Rebecca as a friend. But that doesn't mean you'll chase after her. Maybe in another few days you'll be ready to talk to her again.

At dinner Father announces that the City Tavern will be busy now that the delegates to the Continental Congress are in Philadelphia. He reminds everyone that it is the most elegant dining place in the city. The delegates will arrive in a few days.

"We will all help," Mother says.

To greet the delegates, go to page 55.

To help in the stable, turn to page 63.

You love going to the City Tavern. It smells of coffee and whatever delicacies the cooks are preparing. There are club rooms where groups can meet. Waiters serve meals in the dining rooms. People gather to talk and drink coffee in the coffee room. Father keeps track of it all and makes sure everyone receives excellent service.

Delegates from various colonies arrive in late August. Father likes to greet customers at the door. You stand beside him when a delegation from Massachusetts arrives. The four men and their servants are a bit dusty, and they look tired. "We've been on the road for three weeks," one man says. "Please excuse our appearance."

Father welcomes the men. "My daughter will see you to the dining room," he says.

You lead the way.

Turn the page.

Several gentlemen are already seated in the dining room. They rise to greet the newcomers. Dr. Shippen, Dr. Knox, and Mr. Smith are from Philadelphia. Mr. Linch and Mr. Gadsden are from South Carolina. Mr. Thomas McKean of Delaware arrives soon after. You show him to the dining room too.

Standing aside, you overhear the introductions. The Massachusetts men are Samuel Adams, Thomas Cushing, John Adams, and Robert Treat Paine. Father told you that Samuel Adams probably organized the tea party in Boston.

When Father comes to check on the service, he sees you lingering by the window. "Home with you!" he says.

It's late and you're tired, but you don't want to leave yet.

To go home, turn to page 58.

To ask to stay, turn to page 61.

You dash outside. "Rebecca!" you call. "May I join you?"

Rebecca seems surprised. "I'm taking these muffins to my grandmother's house. You can come if you like."

You walk beside Rebecca. You don't mention Boston or Great Britain or King George, and in time, you both forget about the disagreement.

In a few weeks, the delegates of the Continental Congress come to town. It's an exciting time in Philadelphia. The City Tavern is busy. Father may need your help. An elderly neighbor, Mrs. Kelly, has asked you to deliver her eggs. The boy who usually does it is ill. Which should you do first?

To help Mrs. Kelly, turn to page 67.

To check with Father, turn to page 68.

It's a short walk home. Your sisters have just returned from a quilting party. The girls and four friends are making a quilt—a wedding gift for their friend Fanny. You suspect they did more talking than sewing. Your sisters always come home with interesting gossip.

"George Washington is a delegate," Molly says.

"They say he is tall and handsome." Sara says.

"He's married," Molly replies.

You grin. Sara is eighteen and searching for a husband. You leave the girls and scoot off to bed.

The next day Mother has some errands. She needs ribbons from Miss Smith's shop on Chestnut Street. And Mrs. Kelly, an elderly neighbor, needs someone to deliver eggs to her customers. The boy who usually does it is ill.

To go to the shop for ribbons, turn to page 66.

To deliver eggs, turn to page 67.

You peek into the dining room. Father is deep in conversation with a well-dressed man. You know better than to interrupt him. So you wander into the kitchen. A strange boy is talking with the servants. He sees you and smiles. The head cook pours the boy coffee and offers him a hot muffin. She gives you one too.

"Excuse my dust," the boy says to the cook. "I've been on the road for many days." He speaks with a strange accent. He's not from Philadelphia.

Turn the page.

Express riders delivered important messages throughout the American colonies in the 1700s.

"Mr. Smith will know where you can find Mr. Adams," the cook says, referring to your father.

"Mr. Adams?" you ask.

"Yes. Mr. Samuel Adams. I'm an express rider from Boston. I have a packet of letters for him. I carry messages back and forth."

"Will you take my letter to Boston?" You hold it out to the rider as you explain it is for Nabby Adams, John Adams' daughter.

"Happy to, Miss," he says. He puts the letter into his sack. "I'll make certain that it reaches Miss Adams."

"Now run along," the cook says with a grin. "Your father will not be happy to find you bothering his kitchen staff."

Turn to page 70.

"But Father, can't I stay just a bit longer?"

Father smiles. "I'm proud of you for wanting to help. But go home now, and I'll have a special job for you tomorrow."

A special job? What could it be? You go home, feeling too excited to sleep.

Turn to page 68.

Patrick Henry was a delegate from Virginia at the Continental Congress. In a speech he said, "I am not a Virginian, but an American."

Mr. Adams is staying at a boardinghouse called the Stone House. It's across from the City Tavern. You knock on the door. Mrs. Yard, who owns the house, answers. "Yes?"

"I have a letter for Mr. Adams," you say. "For his daughter. Would you give it to him?"

"Of course. He spends his days in committee meetings," Mrs. Yard says. "The delegates are writing a list of grievances to send to King George. They are hoping the king will want peace with the colonies. No one wants war." Mrs. Yard looks troubled. "Imagine the colonies trying to fight the king's soldiers. They are trained in warfare. Our colonists are mostly farmers or shopkeepers. They are not fighters. I fear we won't have much of a chance if it comes to war." She wipes her face with her apron. "Sorry, child. I should not trouble you with adult concerns. Give me the letter. I'll see that Mr. Adams gets it."

Turn to page 70.

Most of the delegates arrive on horseback or in carriages. You've always been comfortable around the horses. Most city girls are not allowed to muck out the stalls and brush the horses, but Father believes it's honorable work. Asa, who runs the stable, welcomes your help.

You spend an hour or so grooming horses.

"That one belongs to Mr. William Livingston. He's a lawyer from New Jersey. And that one," Asa says, pointing to a chestnut mare, "belongs to Philip Livingston from New York. He's a merchant."

"Are they relatives?" you ask.

"Brothers. They were born in Albany, but William moved to New Jersey and Philip moved to New York City."

Congress meets for several more weeks. You often help Asa in the stable. He loves to talk.

Turn the page.

"Congress is sending a list of grievances to King George," he says.

"Grievances?" you ask.

"Yes," Asa says. "Complaints or protests. The delegates have chosen two members from each colony to put together a list for the king. They call it a report of American rights."

He also tells you what he knows about Mr. Samuel Adams. "They say that he eats little, drinks little, sleeps little, and thinks much. He'll make sure Congress does what he wants."

Congress adjourns in late October. Asa tells you that Congress ordered the colonies to organize militia units and to gather arms and ammunition. He says, "I heard that Mr. Patrick Henry said, 'Arms are necessary and necessary now.'"

"If there's a war . . ." you begin to say, but you don't know how to finish. You don't know much

Samuel Adams was one of the organizers of Boston's Sons of Liberty. He represented Massachusetts at the Continental Congress.

about war, but you're sure that one would change your life in ways you can't imagine. "I hope it doesn't come to that," you say.

"Time will tell," Asa says, shaking his head. "Time will tell."

THE END

To follow another path, turn to page 9.
To read the conclusion, turn to page 101.

You race through the streets to Anne and Jane Howard's milliner shop. They sell all manner of things, including hats, cloaks, and shawls. They also sell gloves, ribbons, and feathers. You pick up the package of ribbons Mother ordered.

"Have you any news?" Miss Howard asks. "About the Congress," she adds.

"George Washington is here. And I met Mr. John Adams and his cousin, Samuel," you reply.

"Ah," she says. "They'll teach King George that he can't treat the colonies unfairly."

You're surprised to hear the dainty Miss Howard speak so boldly.

"They will," you say with a smile. "Good day."

Then you rush home with the ribbons.

THE END

To follow another path, turn to page 9.
To read the conclusion, turn to page 101.

66

It's a short walk to Mrs. Kelly's house. She puts a dozen eggs into your basket. "These are for Mrs. Yard. Her boarding house is called the Stone House. It's right across from the City Tavern. Do you know the place?"

You nod. Mrs. Kelly is a talker. You're eager to make the delivery, but she has more to say. "Mrs. Yard has a full house. Some of the delegates to the Continental Congress are staying there." She puts her hands on her waist proudly. "Just think. My hens will help the Continental Congress," she declares. "They'll tell King George a thing or two." The hens are clucking and fighting over the corn. "Off with you," she says.

You deliver the eggs. Then you race home. You're proud that you are helping too. It's an exciting time in America.

THE END

To follow another path, turn to page 9.
To read the conclusion, turn to page 101.

"There is a way you can help," Father says. "Go to the docks. I've heard rumors a ship carrying British soldiers is arriving today. If so, that's important information. Don't ask, just watch and tell me what you see."

You race to the port. Sometimes Father hires people off the docks to work at the tavern. But today the port seems quiet.

Many ships sailed in and out of Philadelphia every day.

Suddenly several companies of soldiers march to the docks. You recognize the uniforms. These belong to the Royal Regiment of Ireland.

A man standing nearby says, "They marched here from New Jersey. I hear they're going to Boston. You just wait, Missy. There'll be lots of trouble before this is over."

You run back to the tavern and tell your father what you've seen.

"You've done well," he says. "Women and children make the best spies. I'll tell others what you have seen."

From now on, you'll be watchful. Father is right. No one would suspect a girl of being a spy. If war comes you plan to do your part.

THE END

To follow another path, turn to page 9.
To read the conclusion, turn to page 101.

On October 20 Father says that Congress formed a Continental Association. "It calls for a complete ban on trade between America and England," he says. "The delegates will leave soon, but they plan to meet again next May."

You're sorry to see them leave Philadelphia. It was exciting to have the Congress in session.

A week later a letter arrives from Braintree. You read it carefully so as not to tear the thin paper.

After reading the letter, you make a place for it in your treasure box. Tomorrow you'll write to Nabby again. After all, you are not just a girl of Pennsylvania. You're a girl of America.

You pause for a moment, then take the letter out of the box and unfold it. You want to read it one more time.

Dearest Friend,

How exciting to have a friend in Philadelphia. I read your letter with joy. My father will return soon. He writes to Mother almost every day when he is away. She writes to him too.

She says that in times of peace, we must prepare for war. News has arrived that all men between ages 16 and 60 must join the militia and train for war. I have no older brothers, but I worry for others.

When next you write, tell me more about your family. Perhaps someday we will meet.

Your friend,

Nabby Adams

THE END

To follow another path, turn to page 9.
To read the conclusion, turn to page 101.

Patriot recruiters did their best to convince citizens to join the war effort against Great Britain. There was a great need for volunteers to serve in positions such as Continental Army soldiers, sailors, and express riders.

RECRUITING OFFICE

CHAPTER 4

SKIRMISHES AND A DECLARATION

Father runs a stable in Boston. Dr. Joseph Warren, one of Boston's leading patriots, is a good friend. So are Samuel Adams and John Hancock. They are leading protests against the harsh British rule.

"Dr. Warren needs a few good riders with fast horses to carry messages throughout the colonies," Father tells you one day. "Are you interested?"

"Yes, sir!" you reply.

You're 16 and old enough to drill with the militia, but being an express rider sounds even better.

Turn the page.

"You might be asked to ride all the way to Philadelphia," Father says. "Remember your Aunt Sylvie? She married Jacob Graff. You can stay with them."

A few days later, Ebenezer Dorr stops by the stable and speaks to your father. Dorr looks you over and says, "Dr. Warren needs two riders. One will go north and the other will go south. You'll report back to Dr. Warren or me. If we're not available, you can trust William Dawes or Henry Knox."

"Knox the book seller?" you ask. "But I thought—"

"His family is loyal to the king," Dorr says, "but Knox is one of us."

To go north, go to page 75.
To go south, turn to page 76.

"I'll go north," you say.

Dorr hands you a small packet. It's addressed to Colonel John Stark. "Guard it well," Dorr says.

You gather food, a canteen, a fishhook, and twine. You reach Manchester, New Hampshire, 60 miles northeast of Boston, in two days. A farmer points the way to Stark's sawmill.

Colonel Stark reads the letter thoughtfully. "We'll return to Boston in the morning," he says. "General Ward, commander in chief of the patriot army, plans to place cannons in case the British attack. He wants my assistance."

Two days later, as you approach Boston, Stark leaves to meet General Ward. You continue on.

To report to Dorr before going home, turn to page 76.

To go home first, turn to page 77.

"Paul Revere is leaving for Philadelphia. Dr. Warren wants you to go with him," Dorr says.

You leave immediately. You and Revere stop at the homes of patriots along the route to exchange tired horses for fresh ones.

You reach Philadelphia on May 17, 1775, and go directly to the Pennsylvania State House. At the State House a page fetches Samuel Adams. Revere delivers the news. "Ethan Allen and his Green Mountain Boys have captured Fort Ticonderoga from the British."

"Wait here," Adams says. He returns with a packet of letters. "For Boston," he says.

Revere turns to you. "Can you make the trip alone?" he asks. "One of us must return to Boston. The other will wait here. The delegates are bound to have more letters and messages in a few days."

To return to Boston, turn to page 78.

To stay in Philadelphia, turn to page 83.

Mother welcomes you with a hug and a cup of coffee. "Your father is at the stable. He'll want to see you," she says.

Father is upset. "There are nearly 9,000 British soldiers camped in Boston," he says. "There are battleships anchored in the port, and several British generals are advising Governor Gage." He shakes his head before continuing. "But don't stand here listening to me. You must report to Dr. Warren. Oh, and on the way, stop by the militia camp and give this blanket to your brother."

To go see Dr. Warren, turn to page 79.

To go to the army camp, turn to page 94.

"I know the way," you say. After all, you paid close attention on the way to Philadelphia. The return trip to Boston takes another six days. You only make a few wrong turns along the way. You deliver the messages to Dr. Warren.

"Good. We'll send for you when we need your services," he says.

It's hard to wait. Father cautions you to be patient. A few days later Dorr asks you to deliver letters from John Adams to his wife, Abigail, in Braintree, Massachusetts.

Turn to page 84.

Joseph Warren (pictured) sent Paul Revere on his famous "midnight ride" on April 18, 1775.

Dr. Warren lives in an elegant home on Hanover Street. Father tells you that Warren rents the house. "He sent his young children and his fiancée, Miss Mercy Scollay, to Worchester. They are staying with a doctor friend. He thinks they'll be safer there."

William Eustis, who is learning medicine from Dr. Warren, answers the door. "The doctor is in a meeting," he says. "I fear he'll be awhile. Would you like to wait?"

You hesitate, and then you remember Dorr's words: "If Warren is not available, report to me or Henry Knox."

To find Ebenezer Dorr, turn to page 80.

To go to Henry Knox's bookshop, turn to page 82.

You find Dorr at the Green Dragon Tavern. "Dr. Warren wants you to go to Philadelphia with me," Dorr says. "He wants you to learn the route. You'll be on your own next time." He takes a swig of his drink. "Now, go get your horse," he says.

You meet Dorr at Boston Neck and begin the journey. He introduces you to patriots along the route. They give you food, shelter, and fresh horses. In Philadelphia you meet the Massachusetts delegates. They have packets of letters for you to take back to Boston.

You return to Boston a few days after the battle at Bunker Hill. The militia killed hundreds of British officers and soldiers. British losses were higher, but they claimed victory. You're stunned to hear that Dr. Warren died fighting beside the militia. It's a terrible loss.

Patriot leaders keep you busy traveling back and forth between Boston and Philadelphia. You don't always know what is in the messages, but you protect them with your life.

When Congress approves the invasion of the British province of Quebec, you carry the news to Boston. By then General George Washington is in Boston commanding the Continental Army. You spread word of British attacks in Virginia and South Carolina.

A few days later Dorr sends you to Philadelphia again. After you deliver the secret messages, Samuel Adams asks you to stay in Philadelphia. "We need someone to deliver messages right here in the city."

Turn to page 83.

It doesn't take you long to spot Mr. Knox at his bookshop. He looks as if he weighs about 300 pounds. He says that Dorr mentioned you might stop by. Then he hands you a packet of letters. "These letters go to Mrs. Adams in Braintree. Can you find the way?"

"Yes, sir." You hide the letters beneath your shirt and hurry to the stable for a horse.

Turn to page 84.

Henry Knox commanded artillery under George Washington throughout the Revolutionary War.

Aunt Sylvie and her husband, Jacob Graff, live in a house at the corner of Philadelphia's 7th and Market Streets. "Jacob's a bricklayer," Sylvie says. "He built this house. It's too big for us now, but someday—"

"When you have dozens of children?" you ask, which makes her laugh.

"Maybe not dozens," she says. "For now, we are renting the second floor to Mr. Thomas Jefferson of Virginia."

They offer you a small room. "And if you have spare time, I can always use a good worker," Jacob says.

83

Turn to page 86.

You're in Braintree on June 17, 1775, when militia troops and British soldiers clash at Bunker Hill in Boston. You return the next day. The British claim victory. You're stunned to hear that the colonists lost 450 men, including Dr. Joseph Warren.

Dorr meets you at Father's stable. "We must get the news to Philadelphia," he says, handing you a thick packet. "Deliver it to Samuel Adams. William Dawes is going with you."

Dawes dresses like a farmer. You're dressed like a stable boy. When you get to Philadelphia, the doorman refuses to let you enter the State House. It's an elegant building, and you are dirty and sweaty from the journey.

"We may have to wait all day," Dawes says. "Maybe we should stable our horses."

To wait, go to page 85.

To stable the horses, turn to page 93.

You decide to wait. Fifteen minutes later, the delegates take a break for lunch. Dawes nabs Samuel Adams and gives him the message. Adams scans it, his face tinged with grief. "Go stable your horses," he says. "Meet me later at the City Tavern."

You watch delegates come and go outside the tavern. "That's Patrick Henry of Virginia," Dawes says. "He's for independence. He said, 'Give me liberty or give me death.' He's a brave man."

It's late when the Massachusetts delegates arrive. They hand Dawes several letters. "Deliver these to the Massachusetts Assembly," John Hancock says. Then he looks at you. "Plan to stay for a while. We will have need of you here."

You stay with your Aunt Sylvie and her husband, Jacob Graff. Jacob is a mason. "Make yourself at home," Sylvie says. "If the Congress doesn't keep you busy, Jacob will. He's always building something."

Turn to page 86.

The days pass swiftly. Every day you report to the State House in case the Massachusetts delegates have messages for you. If they do, you make deliveries around town. If not, you help Jacob.

You often overhear what's happening in Congress. On May 24 John Hancock is elected president of the Continental Congress. On June 14 Congress agrees to raise a Continental Army. "George Washington will serve as commander in chief," Samuel Adams tells you the next day.

You've seen General Washington in Philadelphia. He's a tall man who always wears a military uniform. You overhear John Adams say, "Washington may be quiet, but his great experience and ability in military matters is of much service to us."

Paul Revere comes from Boston often. "It's good you're staying here," he says. "You're doing your part."

In July you carry notes to John Dickinson of Pennsylvania. He's writing the Olive Branch Petition, a final attempt to make peace with King George.

Congress takes a late summer break. Many go home. You don't. Jacob Graff has plenty of work, and you enjoy life in the big city.

There is a flurry of activity when Congress returns in September. In October you hear that four British navy ships fired on the town of Falmouth, Massachusetts. They destroyed the village. Towns up and down the coast worry about similar attacks.

Turn the page.

Delegates from Rhode Island have been urging Congress to create a navy. Samuel Chase of Maryland says it is "the maddest idea in the world." But the attack on Falmouth quiets the critics. John Adams senses the change. He, too, wants a navy and sends you scurrying with notes to like-minded delegates.

Samuel Adams claps you on the back and says, "We'll have the grandest revolution the world has ever seen." He thinks Congress is being too slow to act. "So many committees." He sighs. "And each one needs a messenger. One group will meet General Washington in Cambridge. John Adams' group will meet here to discuss New Hampshire's request to set up its own government."

To go to Cambridge, go to page 89.

To stay in Philadelphia, turn to page 90.

It will be good to go home. Cambridge is right outside Boston. The trip takes well over a week. Benjamin Franklin of Pennsylvania, Thomas Lynch of South Carolina, and Benjamin Harrison of Virginia travel by carriage. You ride horseback.

The committee goes directly to Washington's headquarters in Cambridge. You can stay in the house they rented or you can go home. "Remember that the city is under tight British control," Franklin warns.

To stay in Cambridge, turn to page 91.

To go home, turn to page 96.

George Washington

You feel loyal to John Adams, so you stay in Philadelphia. It's clear from the beginning that the committee will give New Hampshire permission to form its own government. In November South Carolina forms a government too. "We're moving toward independence," a delegate says.

In January 1776 Thomas Paine publishes a 47-page pamphlet called *Common Sense*. Everyone is reading it.

"Listen to this," Aunt Sylvie says. "Paine writes that 'by an independence, we take rank with other nations.' I vote for independence." Of course, it's Congress who will decide, not Aunt Sylvie.

Turn to page 97.

You'll stay in Cambridge in case the committee needs you. Committee members meet with Washington for seven days. You take notes. Washington complains that the army is undisciplined. The committee decides on punishments, including the death penalty for anyone who refuses to obey orders. They discuss rations: 1 pound of beef, 1 pound of salt fish, or 3/4 pounds of pork per man per day. They intend to increase the army to 20,372 men. You write down the precise numbers. Finally Washington asks that Congress send money. Maintaining an army is costly.

You enjoy helping Dr. Franklin. He's smart and has a good sense of humor. He seems to like you too.

Six months later, Congress sends delegates to Quebec to check on progress there. Dr. Franklin asks you to go along.

Turn the page.

It's a long, cold journey. Some nights you all sleep on the floor of a house destroyed in an earlier battle. Others complain, but not Dr. Franklin. He tells funny stories about his life.

When you finally reach Montreal, you meet General Benedict Arnold. He needs money too. After a week of meetings, Franklin says that if the colonies can't support the army, then it is better if the soldiers are sent home. Soon after, members of Congress agree. They order the troops to withdraw.

In January 1776 Thomas Paine publishes a 47-page pamphlet called *Common Sense*. Paine writes in language everyone can understand. He writes that King George and Parliament should not tell Americans what to do. He declares that America should become independent.

Franklin is delighted. He says that Paine's pamphlet will change everything.

Turn to page 97.

"I'll stable the horses while you wait here," you suggest. "Then we can switch places."

You stable the horses and fill your canteen. It was a long, hot ride. It won't hurt to take a short break. You lie down on the hay and fall into a deep sleep.

It's dark when you wake. You stumble to your feet as Dawes emerges from a stall. His horse is saddled. "I have messages for Boston," he says. "I'm leaving."

"What about me?" you ask.

"Find your own way home," he says.

You've failed. A soldier who falls asleep on duty can be whipped. You are never asked to ride express again. Congress is in session for another year. By the time the colonies declare independence, you're marching with the Massachusetts militia. You'll do your part as a soldier in the fight for independence.

THE END
To follow another path, turn to page 9.
To read the conclusion, turn to page 101.

Your brother, Nathan, and his regiment are camped in Cambridge. The Common was once grazing land for cows. Now it's a patriot army camp.

"We've 20,000 soldiers here," a militiaman tells you. "Good luck finding your brother."

Luck is with you. You find Nathan sitting beside a nearby tent. "Nathan!" you call. Something's wrong. His eyes don't seem to focus, and he's holding his head.

"Headache," he says. "I have the flu. Lots of the men do. Mother will know what to do."

After the Battles of Lexington and Concord, thousands of militiamen gathered on Cambridge Common to await orders.

Nathan's captain gives him leave. "Get well, son," he says. He keeps his distance. He doesn't want to catch whatever Nathan has.

You help Nathan onto your horse. You walk beside him. It's not far.

Mother takes one look at Nathan and helps him to bed. In a few days, his fever drops. The headache and backache go away. But soon after, he develops sores in his mouth, nose, and throat.

"Smallpox," Mother says. She keeps the younger children away, but you've already been exposed. Soon you begin to feel ill. Your symptoms are a lot like Nathan's. Mother sends you to bed. Nathan recovers. Sadly your case is more severe and you never recover. Like many others in Boston during the 1770s, smallpox ends your life.

THE END

To follow another path, turn to page 9.
To read the conclusion, turn to page 101.

Your family is pleased to see you. You stay overnight, but when you try to leave the next day, British guards at Boston Neck stop you. "Passage denied," one says.

It's no use arguing. You try again, but they refuse to let you pass. You're stuck in Boston until March 17, 1776, when the British leave the city. "They're off to New York," a neighbor says.

You rush to Cambridge. General Washington is moving the Continental Army to New York. You sign on. After all, they need brave men to join the fight.

96

THE END

To follow another path, turn to page 9.
To read the conclusion, turn to page 101.

Soon everyone is talking about independence. On June 17 Congress appoints the Committee of Five to draft a declaration. John Adams and Benjamin Franklin are on the committee. So are Robert Livingston of New York, Roger Sherman of Connecticut, and Thomas Jefferson of Virginia.

The next day as you go upstairs to your room, you overhear John Adams and Thomas Jefferson talking. You stop to listen. Jefferson wants Adams to draft the declaration.

"I will not," Adams says.

"You should do it," Jefferson says.

"I will not," Adams repeats.

"What can be your reasons?" Jefferson asks.

Turn the page.

"Reason first, you are a Virginian and a Virginian ought to appear at the head of this business," Adams explains. "Reason second, I am obnoxious, suspected, and unpopular. You are very much otherwise. Reason third, you can write 10 times better than I can."

"Well, if you are decided, I will do as well as I can," Jefferson says.

As Mr. Adams leaves Jefferson's room, he sees you on the stairs.

"Stay nearby," he says. "Mr. Jefferson will need a messenger."

For the next several days, Mr. Jefferson stays at his desk writing. From time to time, he sends you to Benjamin Franklin's house with a draft and a note. The note says, "Will Doctor Franklin be so good as to peruse it?"

Each time you wait while Franklin reads the document, makes a few hasty notes, and sends it back to Jefferson. Seven days later the declaration is finished.

Congress reads it, debates it, edits it, and finally votes to accept it on July 4, 1776. On July 6 John Hancock requests your services. "Deliver the Declaration of Independence to Massachusetts," he says.

You reach for it. "It's an honor, sir."

THE END

To follow another path, turn to page 9.
To read the conclusion, turn to page 101.

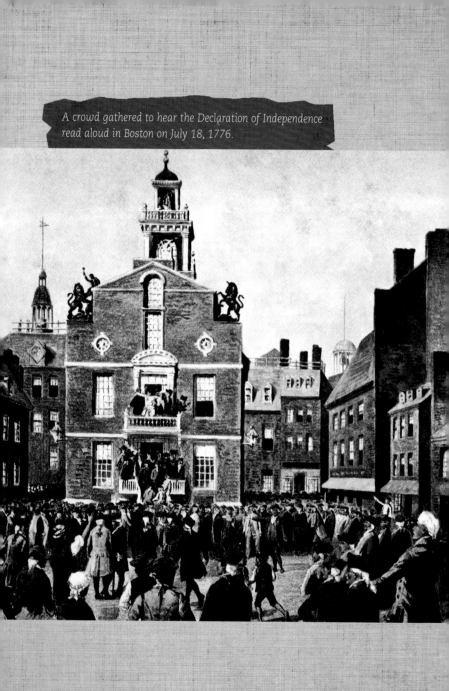

A crowd gathered to hear the Declaration of Independence read aloud in Boston on July 18, 1776.

CHAPTER 5

MOVING FORWARD

The British Parliament's Coercive Acts against Boston angered the colonists. The colonists elected delegates to the First Continental Congress to deal with the matter. Congress met from September 5 to October 26, 1774. Delegates from every colony except Georgia attended. The people in Georgia were too busy dealing with attacks from the Creek tribe along their western border.

Congress had just begun meeting when shots were fired in Lexington and Concord, Massachusetts. No one knows who fired the first shot. Each side claimed it was the other. Despite who fired first, these battles set off a series of events that led to the Revolutionary War.

Fifty years later Massachusetts poet Ralph Waldo Emerson called this moment "the shot heard round the world."

Despite the colonies' grievances, Congress hoped for a peaceful solution to these problems. The delegates sent a list of grievances and a declaration of rights to Britain's King George III. Those rights included life, liberty, and property. When the king did not answer, Congress ordered the colonies to organize militias and to boycott British goods.

On May 10, 1775, the Second Continental Congress gathered in Philadelphia. By then, tension between British forces and American militia had increased. Actual battles had taken place in New England. Tensions were also high in New York, Maryland, Virginia, and Connecticut. A month later, on June 17, 1775, the Battle of Bunker Hill was fought in Boston.

Congress continued to meet throughout 1775 and into 1776. John Dickinson of Pennsylvania wrote the Olive Branch Petition in July 1775. It was a final appeal to King George. The king never responded. In the meantime Congress established an army, a navy, the Marine Corps, and a postal system. Congress approved the invasion of the British province of Quebec—modern-day Canada—by General Benedict Arnold. Congress members feared an attack on the American colonies from British troops in Quebec. They also hoped to convince the northern colonists to join the American cause for independence. A few northerners joined the cause. However, most decided to remain loyal to Great Britain.

In the south colonists captured the British Fort Johnson in South Carolina and defended Hampton, Virginia, from British attack.

Redcoats and patriots clashed on Breed's Hill, at the Battle of Bunker Hill, in 1775.

In January 1776 Thomas Paine published his famous pamphlet, *Common Sense,* which sold a huge number of copies. People everywhere were reading Paine's words. His pamphlet convinced many colonists that rebelling against Britain made good sense.

In June 1776 Congress decided to declare independence from Great Britain. Members appointed the Committee of Five to draft the document. The committee included John

Adams of Massachusetts, Benjamin Franklin of Pennsylvania, Robert Livingston of New York, Roger Sherman of Connecticut, and Thomas Jefferson of Virginia. The committee provided advice, but it was Jefferson who wrote the document. Congress approved the Declaration of Independence on July 4, 1776. Pennsylvania printer John Dunlap made 200 single-sided copies called broadsides. John Hancock sent copies to every colony.

When the declaration was read in Philadelphia, people cheered and lit bonfires. People tore down British flags in some cities. In others people held parades and fired guns into the air. The Declaration of Independence made it clear that America would no longer tolerate British rule. It also gave people hope that America would eventually become a nation based on ideas of equality and rights. These ideas were worth fighting for.

TIMELINE

December 16, 1773—When the colonial governor of Massachusetts refuses to send three shiploads of tea back to Britain, colonists dressed as Mohawk Indians board the ships anchored in Boston Harbor and dump the tea into the water

March–June 1774—The British Parliament passes the Coercive Acts to punish Massachusetts

September 5–October 26, 1774—The First Continental Congress meets in Philadelphia

October 14, 1774—Congress adopts a declaration of rights stating that the colonists are entitled to "life, liberty, and property"

April 14, 1775—British General Thomas Gage, governor of Massachusetts, is ordered to use force to suppress the patriot rebellion

April 18, 1775—Gage sends British soldiers to Concord, Massachusetts, to destroy weapons stored there; Paul Revere and William Dawes spread alarm to colonists

April 19, 1775—First shots of the Revolutionary War are fired at Lexington and Concord

May 10, 1775—Second Continental Congress meets in Philadelphia; Ethan Allen leads colonists to capture British Fort Ticonderoga

May 15, 1775—Congress warns colonies to prepare for war

May 24, 1775—Congress elects John Hancock as its president

June 14–15, 1775—Congress establishes an army with George Washington as commander

June 17, 1775—British win the Battle of Bunker Hill

July 5–8, 1775—Congress attempts to reach agreement with King George III; attempt fails

November 10, 1775—Congress establishes the Marine Corps

November 28, 1775—Congress establishes a navy

May 10, 1776—Congress tells the colonies to form their own governments

June 1–28, 1776—British navy attacks South Carolina

June 11, 1776—Congress appoints one committee to write a Declaration of Independence and another to write the Articles of Confederation

July 4, 1776—Congress adopts the Declaration of Independence

July 12, 1776—Congress accepts the Articles of Confederation, the first constitution of the United States

OTHER PATHS TO EXPLORE

In this book, you've seen how events from the past look different from three points of view. Perspectives on history are as varied as the people who lived it. Seeing history from many points of view is an important part of understanding it. Here are ideas for other Revolutionary War points of view to explore.

+ What would you do about the American colonies if you were a member of the British Parliament? Your country is in debt due in part to the French and Indian wars in America. Is it fair to tax the colonies to help pay for that war? Why or why not? You have a son who is an officer in the British Army. Do you want him to go to war in America?

+ King George III has forbidden expansion into lands west of the Cumberland Mountains, but your family plans to settle on the Kentucky frontier. How will a war with Great Britain affect you? How will it affect the American Indian tribes in the region?

+ You want to remain loyal to King George III. You consider yourself British. Many of your neighbors have turned against you. Are you willing to listen to their side or do you close your ears to their opinions? Will they listen to you? Is dialogue possible when two groups hold such different opinions?

READ MORE

Betti, Matthew. *The Declaration of Independence and the Continental Congress*. New York: PowerKids Press, 2016.

Gilman, Sarah. *The Founding of America*. New York: Enslow, 2017.

Hinman, Bonnie. *The Second Continental Congress*. Hallandale, Fla.: Mitchell Lane Publishers, 2017.

Mara, Wil. *The Battles of Lexington and Concord: Start of the American Revolution*. Lake Elmo, Minn.: Focus Readers, 2017.

INTERNET SITES

Use FactHound to find Internet sites related to this book.

Visit *www.facthound.com*

Just type in 9781543515411 and go.

GLOSSARY

adjourn (uh-JURN)—close or end something

apprentice (uh-PREN-tiss)—someone who learns a trade by working with a skilled person

boycott (BOY-kot)—to refuse to take part in something as a way of making a protest

coerce (koh-URS)—to use force or threats

governor (GUHV-urn-or)—a person who controls a country or state

grievance (GREE-vuhns)—a formal expression of a complaint

intolerable (in-TOL-ur-uh-buhl)—so harsh or bad that it cannot be accepted

loyalist (LOI-uh-list)—a colonist who was loyal to Great Britain during the Revolutionary War

militia (muh-LISH-uh)—group of volunteer citizens organized to fight, but who are not professional soldiers

page (PAYJ)—a person who carries messages and runs errands

Parliament (PAR-luh-muhnt)—the national legislature of Great Britain

patriot (PAY-tree-uht)—a person who sided with the colonies during the Revolutionary War

proprietor (proh-PREYE-uh-ter)—the person in charge of a business establishment, hotel, or restaurant

rebel (REB-uhl)—a person who opposes a government or ruler

BIBLIOGRAPHY

Andrlik, Todd. *Reporting the Revolutionary War: Before It Was History, It Was News.* Naperville, Ill.: Sourcebooks, 2012.

Beck, Derek W. *Igniting the American Revolution: 1773–1775.* Naperville, Ill.: Sourcebooks, 2015.

Brands, H. W. *The First American: The Life and Times of Benjamin Franklin.* New York: Doubleday, 2000.

Cook, Don. *The Long Fuse: How England Lost the American Colonies, 1760–1785.* New York: Atlantic Monthly Press, 1995.

Ellis, Joseph J. *Revolutionary Summer: The Birth of American Independence.* New York: Alfred A. Knopf, 2013.

Ferling, John. *Independence: The Struggle to Set America Free.* New York: Bloomsbury, 2011.

Ferling, John. *Whirlwind: The American Revolution and the War that Won It.* New York: Bloomsbury, 2015.

Harvey, Robert. *"A Few Bloody Noses": The Realities and Mythologies of the American Revolution.* Woodstock, N.Y.: Overlook Press, 2002.

Meacham, Jon. *Thomas Jefferson: The Art of Power.* New York: Random House, 2012.

Middlekauff, Robert. *The Glorious Cause: The American Revolution, 1763–1789.* New York: Oxford University Press, 2005.

Platt, John R. *The City Tavern: Independence National Historical Park, Philadelphia, Pennsylvania.* Denver, Colo.: National Park Service, 1973.

Taylor, Alan. *American Revolutions: A Continental History, 1750–1804.* New York: W. W. Norton, 2016.

INDEX